3 1994 01545 6863

SANTA ANA PUBLIC LIBRARY

AR PTS: 0.5

D0686874

EDGE BOOKS™

Legends of Rock

AEROSMITH
Living the Rock 'n' Roll Dream

J 920 STA
Stark, William N.
Aerosmith

$27.32
CENTRAL   31994015456863

By William N. Stark

Consultant: Meredith Rutledge-Borger,
Associate Curator
Rock and Roll Hall of Fame & Museum
Cleveland, Ohio

CAPSTONE PRESS
a capstone imprint

Edge Books are published by Capstone Press,
1710 Roe Crest Drive, North
Mankato, Minnesota 56003
www.capstonepub.com

Copyright © 2015 by Capstone Press, a Capstone imprint.
All rights reserved. No part of this publication may be
reproduced in whole or in part, or stored in a retrieval
system, or transmitted in any form or by any means,
electronic, mechanical, photocopying, recording, or otherwise,
without written permission of the publisher.

Library of Congress Cataloging-in-Publication Data
Stark, William N., author.
   Aerosmith : living the rock 'n' roll dream / by William N.
Stark.
         pages cm.—(Legends of rock)
   Includes bibliographical references and index.
   Summary: "Describes the rise to fame and the lasting
impact of the band Aerosmith"—Provided
by publisher.
   ISBN 978-1-4914-1815-4 (library binding)
   ISBN 978-1-4914-1820-8 (ebook pdf)
1. Aerosmith (Musical group)—Juvenile literature.
2. Rock musicians—United States—Juvenile literature. I. Title.
   ML3930.A17S73 2015
   782.42166092'2—dc23 [B]   2014023792

Editorial Credits
Mandy Robbins, editor; Tracy Davies-McCabe, designer; Eric
Gohl, media researcher; Gene Bentdahl, production specialist

Direct Quote Sources:
p. 4, http://www.rollingstone.com/music/news/aerosmith-
in-turmoil-behind-the-story-20091130; p. 8, *Circus* Magazine,
1975; p. 15, **Furness, Matters.** *Aerosmith-Uncensored on the
Record.* Coda Books Ltd., 2012; p 19, http://www.mtv.com/
bands/a/aerosmith/news_feature_041702/index7.jhtml; p. 29
(top), Stephen Davis. *Watch You Bleed: The Saga of Guns N'
Roses.* Gotham;, 2008. p. 29 (bottom),
http://www.rockthisway.de/celebrityquotes.htm

Photo Credits
Alamy: Pictorial Press Ltd, 23, S.I.N., 19; AP Photo: Bebeto
Matthews, 26-27; Getty Images: Michael Ochs Archives,
6, 7, 11, 14, Michael Ochs Archives/Ron Pownall, 16-17,
Paul Natkin, 18, Redferns/Fin Costello, 4, 12, Redferns/
Mick Hutson, cover, Redferns/Richard E. Aaron, 13, 22,
WireImage/Jeffrey Mayer, 5, 9, 15; Newscom: Mirrorpix,
24-25, ZUMA Press/Angela Vinci, 20, 21; Shutterstock:
Julius Kielaitis, 10, Yulia Grigoryeva, 28

Design Elements: Shutterstock

Printed in the United States of America in
Stevens Point, Wisconsin.
092014   008479WZS15

Table of Contents

Introduction

The Hair Band

> I think one of the most valuable things Aerosmith has is the energy we produce when we all play together.
>
> —Joe Perry of the band Aerosmith

Tight pants, bare chests, colorful scarves, and big hair defined the Aerosmith look. High-pitched vocals and howling guitars brought fans out by the thousands. Aerosmith screeched onto the music scene in the 1970s and changed rock 'n' roll forever. Hit after hit topped the charts, including "Dream On" (1973), "Walk this Way" (1975 and 1986), and "Crazy" (1993). Soon other bands began copying their signature style. But while other bands rose to fame following the Aerosmith look and sound, Aerosmith fell apart. Friendships broke apart. Bad choices brought trouble. By the early 1980s, the band all but disappeared. Several years later apologies and rehabilitation inspired the greatest comeback in music history. For their talent and hard work, Aerosmith is considered a legend in rock 'n' roll music.

Aerosmith in concert, 1974

Aerosmith Top 10

1. "Dream On"
2. "Sweet Emotion"
3. "Walk This Way"
4. "Back in the Saddle"
5. "I Don't Want to Miss a Thing"
6. "Seasons of Wither"
7. "Mama Kin"
8. "Janie's Got a Gun"
9. "Last Child"
10. "What It Takes"

(according to a *Rolling Stone* magazine readers poll)

French Fries and Music History

Steven Tyler started his first serious band at 16 years old in Sunapee, New Hampshire. The band was called Chain Reaction. Steven gained a reputation for his high-pitched, raspy vocals. At that time, guitarist Joe Perry worked as a cook at a small hamburger and ice cream shop. Steven sometimes ate there. One day he was so impressed by the French fries he ordered that he wanted to meet the cook who made them. Steven went into the kitchen. There stood 19-year-old Joe, the fry cook.

Backstage Pass:

Steven Tyler

Born: March 26, 1948, Yonkers, New York

Role: lead singer and harmonica player

What he brought to the group: Steven Tyler is world famous for his vocal range, including high-pitched screaming that is on key. He has an uncanny ability to harmonize with Joe Perry's guitar and sing nonsense words called "scatting."

Steven Tyler's (far left) early band, Chain Reaction

When Steven and Joe first met, Joe played lead guitar with a group called Jam Band. One evening both young men's bands played at the same place. That night Steven decided to join Joe and his bassist, Tom Hamilton, onstage. The three of them thought they sounded good together and had good chemistry. Steven, Joe, and Tom decided to form their own musical group. Later the trio added a drummer, Joey Kramer, and a rhythm guitarist, Brad Whitford. This was the beginning of Aerosmith.

"I loved joe's style. He always played out of tune and real sloppy and I just loved it."

—Steven Tyler

Backstage Pass:
· ·

Joe Perry

Born: September 10, 1950,
             Lawrence, Massachusetts
Role: guitar player
What he brought to the group:
Joe Perry is a master lead
guitarist who can bend the
strings to Tyler's vocals and
create **riffs** that stand on
their own merits.

riff: a short, rhythmic line of notes that is often
         repeated throughout a song

What's in a Name?

Joey Kramer came up with the Aerosmith name. He based it on doodles of wings and words he'd made on his school notebooks. Some of the band members didn't like it because they didn't like the book *Arrowsmith*, by Sinclair Lewis. They had been required to read it in high school. But Joey's doodle won them over. The musicians called themselves Aerosmith. The band's signature symbol, wings, was a nod to "aero," which is a Greek word meaning "air."

Backstage Pass:

Tom Hamilton

Born: December 31, 1951, Colorado Springs, Colorado
Role: bass guitar player
What he brought to the group: Tom Hamilton is considered an incredibly creative bass guitar player. His work on the Aerosmith tune "Sweet Emotion" is considered some of the finest bass playing in rock 'n' roll.

Backstage Pass:

Brad Whitford

Born: February 23, 1952, Winchester, Massachusetts
Role: guitar player
What he brought to the group: Considered a perfect complement to Joe Perry, Brad Whitford is the technical part of Aerosmith's guitar brain. He also adds warmth and stability to Aerosmith's often high-flying and stormy songs and delivery.

Aerosmith, 1975, from left to right:
top row-Joey Kramer, Tom
Hamilton, Brad Whitford
bottom row-Steven Tyler, Joe Perry

Backstage Pass:

Joey Kramer

Born: June 21, 1950, New York
City, New York

Role: Drummer

What he brought to the group:
Joey Kramer keeps Aerosmith
rhythmically united as the
drummer. With booming beats
and steady precision, Kramer is
the heartbeat of the band.

2 Living and Working Together

In 1970 Aerosmith took up residence in a tiny Boston, Massachusetts, apartment. The young men were broke even though they played every night. They ate next to nothing. All their money went to whatever necessities they needed for the band. When they weren't performing, the band members wrote songs. Joe fooled around on his guitar and recorded riffs onto cassette tapes. Then he passed the cassettes on to Steven. Steven used the recorded riffs to create lyrics to songs. Then the whole band practiced the songs together. Steven's voice ranged from soft and low for tender love songs to high and shrieking for playful **refrains**.

Joe Perry, Tom Kramer, and Brad Whitford tune up backstage before a 1976 concert.

refrain: a regularly repeated part of a song

Attracting Fans

Tom Hamilton once said, "I never really cared about vocals until I was in this band. I always thought vocals were there so the girls would listen." Girls did listen. But so did many other people. Aerosmith quickly gained a following in the Boston area.

Fans flocked not only to hear Steven sing, but also to watch him dance. They enjoyed when he pretended to dance with his mic stand. They loved when he got up close and personal with fans in the front rows. They enjoyed watching him interact with his band members. Steven was a performer in every sense of the word. The onstage energy brought more fans.

In the early-1970s, Aerosmith began playing in New York City. One night famous record producer Clive Davis heard the group for the first time. He signed Aerosmith to Columbia Records, the premier recording label, in 1972. This record deal gave the group their first big break. Aerosmith was launched into stardom.

Clive Davis

"Aerosmith is what rock 'n' roll is all about and has been from its inception to the present day." Jimmy Page of the band Led Zeppelin

The ballad "Dream On," a single from Aerosmith's first album, became one of the band's best-loved songs. The band toured from coast to coast. They released another record, *Get Your Wings*, in 1974. It was only a minor success. But it kept the Aerosmith momentum going. In 1975 the band's third album, *Toys in the Attic*, made Aerosmith a household name. People loved hits such as "Sweet Emotion" and "Walk this Way." Aerosmith headlined some of the largest venues in the country. They filled those spaces to capacity.

Dreams Gone Wrong

After several years, though, the members of Aerosmith started to feel smothered by each other. The group traveled together in a bus. They ate together, practiced together, and played together for months on end. Constant travel in close quarters strained relationships. The band members, especially Steven and Joe, got on each other's nerves. Even the band members' girlfriends got to fighting. Some members began abusing drugs and alcohol. Aerosmith started to unravel by the end of the 1970s.

Aerosmith, 1978

Toxic TWINS

"Toxic Twins" was a nickname given to Steven and Joe for their bad-boy ways and serious drug and alcohol abuse. At times Steven and Joe appeared to embrace the handle. Even though their antics attracted negative attention, Aerosmith's fan base grew. But Steven and Joe's bad behaviors damaged their relationship, which hurt the band.

Steven wanted Joe as his musical collaborator and his best friend. But Joe was a loner. He didn't want to devote that much time to Steven. Joe liked to create guitar riffs, or licks, for Steven to write songs around. But he didn't want to be the constant sidekick that Steven seemed to want.

Steven Tyler and Joe Perry rocking out at a 1982 Aerosmith concert

"It's always been a little sad for me with Joe, in that I get the lick, but I don't get that full-time friend."

—Steven Tyler

After years of turmoil, Joe and Brad quit Aerosmith in 1979. They started a new band, The Joe Perry Project. Aerosmith replaced Joe with Jim Crespo and Brad with Rick Dufay. Neither band did very well, though. Without the chemistry between Steven and Joe, it seemed the life had been drained out of Aerosmith.

By the early 1980s, quite a few "hair bands" had copied Aerosmith's look and style. Fans flocked to these new bands, since the original band they loved seemed to have lost its spark. It looked like Aerosmith was poised to fade out of the spotlight altogether.

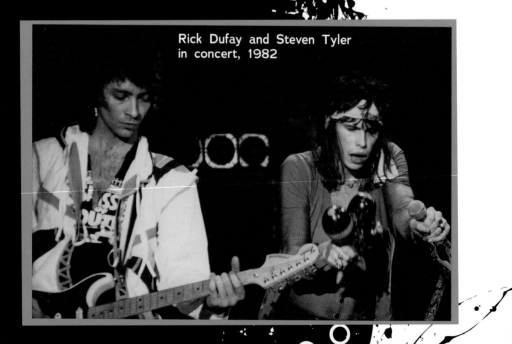

Rick Dufay and Steven Tyler in concert, 1982

Joe Perry on guitar, 1981

4 Recovery and Forgiveness

For several years Aerosmith and The Joe Perry Project focused on different goals. Steven and Joe didn't even speak to each other. Then one night in Boston in 1984, Joe and Brad showed up backstage at an Aerosmith concert. They had a friendly conversation with Steven and realized how much they missed one another. Steven and Joe decided to work together again. They got the whole band back together. The original five members of Aerosmith released the album *Done with Mirrors* in 1985. But the album didn't live up to fans' expectations. It seemed like the band would fade out again.

Joe and Steven, together again, 1984.

Another Chance

In 1986 Aerosmith got a little help from a hip-hop group,
Run-D.M.C. Run-D.M.C. liked Aerosmith's song "Walk this Way."
They created a hip-hop interpretation of it, complete with record
scratches. The song was a huge hit. Suddenly, Aerosmith found a
new and younger audience.

The new interest breathed life back into the band. The remake
of their song also reintroduced Aerosmith to a powerful mode of
dissemination: the music video. In the music video for the hip-hop
version of "Walk This Way," Aerosmith performs on one side of
a wall. Run-D.M.C. performs the same song on the other. Finally,
Steven breaks down the wall. The two bands unite.

Run-D.M.C., 1986, from left to right: Jason Mizell, Darryl McDaniels, and Joseph Simmons

The boost from Run-D.M.C. helped Aerosmith revive its flair for creativity. Aerosmith's work with Run-D.M.C. marked one of the most successful **crossovers** in music history.

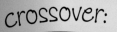 **crossover:** when an artist tries a new genre, or style, of music

In 1987 Aerosmith released their most popular album yet. *Permanent Vacation* solidified the band as one of the greatest musical groups of all time. The songs "Rag Doll," "Dude (Looks Like a Lady)," and "Angel" were enormous hits. The songs displayed Aerosmith's versatility. In a love song, the band peeled back the mysteries of emotion. In the next song, they demonstrated their wit with a fun-filled ditty about cross-dressing. With music videos on MTV, Aerosmith transferred their onstage showmanship to a much larger audience.

Chart Topper: "Dream On"

Steven Tyler wrote the song "Dream On," one of rock 'n' roll's long-enduring anthems. The song holds a special place in Steven's heart because he uses his "real" voice to sing it. Tyler often imitates the styles of various singers, from opera singers to rappers. But in "Dream On," the vocals are authentic Steven Tyler. He sings from the depths of his soul with some of the most powerful vocal cords in music history.

Aerosmith performs at the 1994 MTV Music Awards.

anthem: a song that unites a group of people

In the 1990s albums such as *Get a Grip, Nine Lives*, and *Just Push Play* charmed another decade of critics and fans. A whole new **generation** fell in love with Aerosmith's powerful, gritty sound.

Aerosmith's influence is abundant and far-reaching. Few bands can say that they have both grandmothers and high school students enjoying their music. Considering that the band has a history spanning 40 years, it is not surprising. Fans copied Aerosmith's style in clothing and hair. Musicians copied Aerosmith's style in stage presence and sound. In 2001 Aerosmith was inducted into the Rock and Roll Hall of Fame for the group's lasting contributions to rock music.

Aerosmith performing in
Moscow, Russia, in 2014

—Nikki Six of the band Mötley Crüe

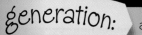 generation: a group of people born around the same time

Glossary

anthem (AN-thuhm)—a song that unites a group of people

ballad (BAL-uhd)—a song or poem that tells a story

capacity (kuh-PASS-uh-tee)—the maximum amount that something can hold

collaborator (kuh-LAB-uh-rayt-uhr)—a person who works with another person

crossover (KROS-oh-vher)—an artist or recording that appeals to more than one portion of a large audience

dissemination (dih-sem-ih-NAY-shuhn)—the act of spreading information

generation (jen-uh-RAY-shuhn)—a group of people born around the same time

refrain (rih-FRAYN)—a regularly repeated part of a song

rehabilitation (ree-huh-bil-uh-TAY-shun)—therapy that helps people recover their health or abilities

reputation (rep-yuh-TAY-shuhn)—a general state in which a person or thing is held by the public

riff (RIF)—a short, rhythmic line of notes that is often repeated throughout a song

venue (VEN-yoo)—a place where an event is held

Read More

Burlingame, Jeff. *Aerosmith: Hard Rock Superstars*. Rebels of Rock. Berkeley Heights, N.J.: Enslow, 2011.

Farseth, Erik. *American Rock: Guitar Heroes, Punks, and Metalheads*. American Music Milestones. Minneapolis: Twenty-First Century Books, 2013.

Greve, Tom. *A Listen to Rock 'n' Roll*. Vero Beach, Fla.: Rourke Educational Media, 2013.

Internet Sites

FactHound offers a safe, fun way to find Internet sites related to this book. All of the sites on FactHound have been researched by our staff.

Here's all you do:

Visit *www.facthound.com*

Type in this code: 9781491418154

Super-cool stuff! Check out projects, games and lots more at **www.capstonekids.com**

Ind£x